AIKIDO

An Introduction To

Tomiki-Style

Randori-No-Kata
& Variations

By

M. J. Clapton

Published by Paul H. Crompton Ltd.,
102 Felsham Road, London, SW15 1DQ England
North America: Talman Company,
131 Spring Street, New York, N.Y. 10012, USA

First Edition 1975

Reprinted 1975

Reprinted 1995

Reprinted 1996

Copyright © MJ Clapton 1974

Design and Artwork by James Dumas Creative Services Ltd
(*based on author's suggestions*)

Printed in Finland by Gummerus Printing,
Jyväskylä

CONTENTS

PREFACE 5

INTRODUCTION 7

    What is Randori-No-Kata

KATA GROUPS OR SECTIONS 10

PREPARATORY NOTES 12

HOW SHOULD THE KATA BE DEMONSTRATED? 14

ATEMI WAZA 18

HIJI WAZA 30

TEKUBI WAZA 42

UKI WAZA 52

VARIATIONS 60

IN CONCLUSION 83

PREFACE

The title of this book will convey to the reader that it is an introduction to the Tomiki-Style of Aikido. The Kata explained in these pages is regarded as the basic Kata of the style — basic insofar as it is *the* main and most commonly practised Kata. As, at the time of writing, there is no other book available on this Kata it is most probable that this style of Aikido is somewhat of an unknown — and misunderstood — sport. Although other books have been published on this style they detail a group of fifteen techniques which were replaced in the early 1960s with the present Randori-No-Kata of seventeen techniques which brought about the present *randori* practised in this style.

This Kata by no means exhausts the techniques of the Tomiki-Style; there are the countering applications — *Kaeshi Waza* — the balance breaking demonstrations — *Happon Katas* — which have been re-named *Shichi Hon Katas* as someone decided that the balance could not really be broken in eight directions but only seven (which is rather a silly presumption) and the Old Style Katas — *Koryu Katas* — which altogether number of 140 techniques.

The reader familiar with other books on either Judo or Aikido will note some omissions from this text.

Anyone with an iota of sense will realise that a thorough knowledge of breakfalling is required before any of these applications can be safely practised. The inclusion of attempted teaching of *ukemi* would only be a waste of space and effort. In this style of Aikido, and I cannot offer comment on other styles because of limited knowledge, the falls or throws are not what they might appear to be. Many *falls* are actually *escapes* which are made by Uke to avoid injury and for this reason ukemi is best left to competent teaching in the dojo.

The History of Aikido has been gone into in occasional lengthy form by others and another variation on that theme would not serve any useful purpose — especially as this style can never really make up its mind as to its history. Over the past fourteen years I have heard four different versions from four eminent Japanese instructors. By trying to ascertain who did what and when they did it serves no useful purpose. To say that Kenji Tomiki was once a pupil of Morehei Uyeshiba, formulated his own style and that Aikido has been developed from *Jujitsu* should serve as sufficient history.

The all-too-familiar section of *self-defence* has been omitted without any second thought or reluctance, perhaps to the disappointment of many. We are all familiar with the two gentlemen attired in lounge suits and shoe-less who get into awful predicaments in either the dojo, the gents washroom or the bar and face untold horrors of rubber knives and toy pistols and emerge triumphant. Perhaps television, motion pictures and the ill-informed media in general have forced us into reading too much into the *Martial* and not enough into the *Art*. Of course, many Aikido applications can be adapted for self-preservation purposes but to imply that a particular technique could and should be used if someone tries to kick sand in your face is rather committal. I would not like to mislead the reader by including 'real life' situations in this text so I leave such gimmicks to those who feel the need for them.

As far as this style is concerned I have omitted the *Basic Movements* which are common in most dojos. As a student I always had to try hard to keep a straight face when I was forced to indulge in these movements and they never fail to raise a giggle or two when they are practised in front of spectators. The waving of arms like a policeman trying to direct large volumes of traffic is not necessary to any practise of Aikido and this style is no exception. Their meaning is a frequent unexplained quantity and many instructors try explaining their practise as being necessary before anyone can learn techniques — *rubbish*. To the Dan Grade learning the Koryu Katas these movements are of interest but to the average student they are an unknown quantity, and an unnecessary quantity.

M.J. Clapton
Stockwell Aikido Club. May 1974

INTRODUCTION

This book deals with *one* of the *Katas* of the *Tomiki-Style* of Aikido, plus combinations and variations relative to the techniques of that Kata for use in either *randori* or free-style practise (*ka kari geiko*).

There is the great mis-belief in this style of Aikido that everything *must* be done in a particular way — that this foot *must* be placed here and this arm *must* be held here. There seems to be little allowance for the individual's capability of the variations in height, weight, speed and individual style of movement. What is a good application to one may well be totally useless to another.

The *kata* details explained in these pages are *basic* details but in free-practise one can and should vary application depending upon the type of person one is practising with. The Tomiki-Style is very basic in its free-style; perhaps because of this belief that everything *must* be done in a certain way, or, perhaps, because variations are not taught because of an instructor's own limited knowledge.

There may well be some discussion amongst devotees of this style about the techniques included in these pages, if not about the actual *kata*. If such discussion does come about then at least some students will be taking some notice and it is hoped will start experimenting for themselves.

There is the tendency to take one instructor as 'gospel' and to disregard the methods of others. No two instructors teach the same and there is a wealth to be learned by visiting various dojos. By taking the best points from various instructors one can form one's own opinions and methods — this sometimes leads to another school within a style but usually this does more good than harm.

The Tomiki-Style is one that is usually misunderstood. Mainly because there is little to which one can refer for guidance. Perhaps this is because this style of Aikido fills, to a certain extent, the gap between Judo and Karate. Such a gap is not explainable either in a few words or within the text of this book. Aikido is one sport that is very misleading. To 'see' an Aikido technique is one thing, but to 'feel' one is a different experience. Visitors to dojos, regardless of style, rarely make allowances for so many aspects to which one must pay respect that are essential to either the instructor's methods or are part of the essential practise of Aikido. It is rather like visiting a Karate dojo, seeing the class going through warming-up exercises and then leaving with the impression that one has 'seen' Karate. There is little appreciation for the simple move and the realisation of the degree of difficulty that may be involved in that move.

The powers of 'ki' and the flowing of thoughts here and there are matters that have been gone into at some length by many others. My personal opinion is that no superhuman effort of Buddhist principle is required — no more ability is required to 'succeed' at Aikido than the effort to kick a football or swing a tennis racquet. Success at Judo and Karate are brought about by competent instruction and hard work — Aikido is no exception.

There are those who argue that the Tomiki-Style is not true Aikido. Of those who do state such things I do not know of any who have spent any real time practising and studying the sport that they criticise. Whatever style, Aikido is Aikido — perhaps we can all learn a little from each other. I hope that this text on the Tomiki-Style might serve that aim, just a little.

WHAT IS RANDORI-NO-KATA?

All who practise a Martial Art will know what *Kata* is; a pre-arranged form of exercise which is usually given a title to denote what the Kata is supposed to represent. It is surprising the number of students, and instructors, of this style who do not know what *Randori-No-Kata* is.

I once asked a student, of relative high grade, from another school what Randori-No-Kata was. As he desired a change from the school that he had been practising with my question received a blank, questioning look that seemed to say, 'some instructor, doesn't even know what it is.' I assured him that I knew what it was but I did not want to teach grandma to suck eggs, so to speak. He informed me that Randori-No-Kata was the basic techniques of Aikido and that all techniques practised were variations of that Kata. Regrettably so very many students of this style are of that same impression and that impression is wrong. Of course, no blame can be attached to a student if he has been misled by an instructor or if he has formed opinions without asking questions. Blame, if any is due, should be attributed to instructors — if one is going to teach one should have an inquiring mind if one's pupils are to receive adequate instruction.

If we are to learn, practise and demonstrate any Kata or any group of techniques we should first understand what that Kata or group is and what it is meant to represent. There is a frequent answer to 'why' questions in this style; that answer is, 'because they do it in Japan'. To the gullible this is the ultimate answer, 'they do it in *Japan*', what more do we need to know! That answer is a reasonable stick but a very bad crutch. Perhaps it serves more as an excuse than a reason.

So, let us try, at least, to understand what this Kata is and what is is supposed to represent, as it is the most common of the style Katas.

In Randori-No-Kata there are seventeen techniques. Why seventeen? Why not seven or twenty-seven? This Kata represents the *basic* techniques used in free-practice, or randori. In *randori* there are seventeen ways in which an opponent can attack, move, react — theoretically there is one application for each reaction or move, combined with height, weight, build etc.

Randori-No-Kata is, therefore, *the basic techniques of free-practice*, or randori, and not the basic techniques of Aikido. The basic techniques of Aikido are the *Koryu Katas*, or Old Style forms as the Tomiki-Style calls them. All of the Randori-No-Kata techniques are variations of one or more of some of these Koryu techniques; the large movement pruned so that a fast application can be made with a minimum amount of movement-wasting time. The application of Koryu techniques are not large in this style by comparison with other styles but as far as the general practice of the style is concerned they are large in practice.

Having established what Randori-No-Kata is we must now try to interpret those three words and we can best grasp their translation and combined meaning if we do so in reverse order.

KATA most students will know that this is a group of techniques which are prearranged to demonstrate a particular facet of the art. But we do have to take another translation to understand the real meaning of kata. If we take the misused term of 'Samurai Sword' we have *Katana*, which means single edge (sword). *Kata*, single edged or *one sided*. If we now take the accepted translation of *Kata* as a prearranged form of exercise and add the *one-sided* additional translation we have a more accurate translation; namely, a prearranged exercise on one side, or, a prearranged *demonstration* performed on one side.

NO this word is a prefix, rather like the Franch à la, or our as per, or resembling.

RANDORI of course, this means free-practice; where one attempts to apply techniques on an opponent when that opponent is trying to apply techniques — regrettably so many mistake *randori* for *shai*.

If we take our translations we come up with several variations, each resulting in the same meaning.

A demonstration of free-practice on one side; a one-sided presentation of free-style; a demonstration on one side resembling free-practice. Whichever one we take we come back to the same basic meaning. If we take a far broader interpretation we have Randori-No-Kata as the basic techniques of free-practice grouped together in an understandable form representing a demonstration of free-practice on one side. The 'one side' not only applying to applications being on one side but there being one Uke and one Tori throughout the Kata. The Kata should, of course, be practised on both sides and in varying sequence so as to become as fully conversant with sequence as possible.

So, we should now know what Randori-No-Kata means and what it is supposed to represent. We must now know what types of techniques are included in the Kata.

KATA GROUPS OR SECTIONS

In this style of Aikido all Katas are grouped into sections. In the Old Style Katas these sections are usually defined according to the type of technique applied by Tori, such as Suwari Waza, Tachi Waza etc. or where the type of application by Tori is mixed they are either according to the type of entry made by Uke, such as Yoko Men Uchi or Ryote Mochi, or, simply group A, B, C etc.

In this Kata they are defined according to the type of application by Tori. All are Tachi Waza so the applications are defined a little more deeply by classifying the part of Uke that is being 'attacked' in defence.

Section A — ATEMI WAZA — Attacking Techniques
          B — HIJI WAZA — Elbow Techniques
          C — TEKUBI WAZA — Wrist Techniques
          D — UKI WAZA — Floating Techniques

Atemi Waza — this group has the most misleading title. It does not imply that Tori actually attacks Uke by striking but the application is in the *form* of an attack that causes Uke to lose balance and by application of *tsugi-ashi* (succeeding foot movements almost identical to those used in kendo) makes Uke fall; in this section, always onto his back.

Hiji Waza — this group entails the use of Uke's elbow joint and shoulder joint to take him to the ground for submission.

Tekubi Waza — in this section the wrist/forearm joints are used to take Uke to the ground for submission.

Uki Waza — in this final section Uke's attack is used as a weapon against him. Tori 'floats' Uke to his rear, rear corner, and direct front and by controlling that floating action causes him to fall.

So that we might understand a little more about the techniques in these groups or sections let us look in a little detail at the techniques; giving their Japanese names and the English translation and I will add a little personal opinion about each application before the technique and the movements of that technique are explained in detail.

I have mentioned about the technique being relevant to the type of 'attack' or entry made by Uke, complying with Uke's reactions; preceding the technique narrative of each section there is a summary of Uke's reactions — namely, the technique is applicable when Uke makes those moves or reactions. The part that Uke has to play is a frequently overlooked point when practising this Kata. Although throughout the Kata Uke makes an 'attack' when one comes to practising *randori* one rather goes on the offensive and uses the techniques as an attack against an opponent. This does somewhat go against the basic principles of Aikido. This is a point that is frequently raised by many Aikidoka (and I do agree with them, believe it or not, perhaps because I do not really like *randori*), but freestyle is the main difference between Tomiki-Style and others. If there are those who are adamant about there being no place for *randori* in Aikido then the answer to them is an obvious one — do not practise the style. However, the style of *randori* is one that is best seen in the dojo and really the written word cannot explain how to practise *randori* in Aikido but should there be those anxious to try then pick yourself an opponent and have him attempt a straight Shomen Ate on you — then defend with any of the seventeen applications, he will then attempt to defend against your applications and so on. But do not turn it into a free-for-all, keep it relaxed and do not be frightened to fall over; it might dent your pride a little but it is *randori* and not *shai* — breakfall practice is something that we all cannot have too much of.

PREPARATORY NOTES

ATEMI WAZA

Attacking Techniques

1.......Shomen Ate or Chin Attack. This is also frequently referred to as Frontal Attack. In kata form it is a technique of reasonably large movement but in variation form it can be cut down and can be very effectively applied with hard force.

2.......Ai Gamae Ate or Regular Posture Attack. The regular posture refers to the postures of Uke and Tori — namely right to right or left to left. These techniques fall into the same category as the *Irimi Nage* applications of other styles. Because the chin is 'attacked' in this application many refer to the variations as Shomen techniques but this is really incorrect. Shomen applications are those that are made *inside* the attacking arm with the opponent's chin being attacked.

3.......Gyaku Gamae Ate or Reverse Posture Attack. Once again, the comparative postures of both parties applies. In free-style the application of this technique in Kata form is a little too delicate to be used with any confidence as the attack is in the facial region and one is likely to strike the eyes. In variation form there are effective variations.

4.......Gedan Ate or Low Position Attack. The low position refers to the area of Uke that is being attacked; in this instance it is the hips. Not very effective in kata form but there are some very hard variations.

5.......Ushiro Ate or Rear Attack. This title refers to the area of Uke being attacked. In kata form it looks a very ineffective application but if the timing is correct it actually works (the author has used this very application in real-life and it has nasty results).

HIJI WAZA

Elbow Techniques

6.......Oshi Taoshi or Push Down. This is where Uke's elbow joint is used by Tori to take him to the ground for submission. The Kata application calls for perfect timing without which the application is non-effective.

7.......Ude Gaeshi or Arm Turn. Although classed as Hiji Waza this application uses the shoulder joint more than the elbow. It is used as a combination to Oshi Taoshi and the arm is turned, causing Uke to fall onto his back. Because of the arm entanglement it is one application that cannot be easily completed with an arm or shoulder lock.

8.......Hiki Taoshi or Pull Down. In this Kata application the elbow joint is levered against and Uke is taken to the ground. In free-style the elbow joint is rarely used; a two-handed grip is applied to the wrist and a hard pull takes Uke down. This variation applied on an inexperienced person can cause severe neck injury and should be applied with some caution.

9......Ude Hineri or Arm Turn. Like Ude Gaeshi above this application uses the shoulder joint to counter resistance to Hiki Taoshi. The 'fall' made by Uke is not an actual throw but like so many Aikido 'throws' is an escape to avoid injury.

10......Waki Gatame or Side Lock. Probably the most complicated and drawn-out of the Kata techniques to perform but in variation it can be cut down and there are some nasty and very effective variations. The application is best 'felt' if Uke remains in an upright posture.

TEKUBI WAZA

Wrist Techniques

11......Kote Hineri or Forearm Twist. This is a very little used application. The technique is intended to take advantage of extended fingers and requires a very fast application by Tori.

12......Kote Gaeshi or Forearm Turn. This application will be known to all Aikido devotees, regardless of style. This application is basically different to that of other styles and most Tomiki-Schools tend to regard their application as sacred, which it most certainly is not. But regardless of style it is one of the most widely used applications.

13......Tenkai Kote Hineri or Turning Forearm Twist. This technique in the application of the Forearm Twist is actually Gyaku Kote Hineri. Many students refer to it as 'Tenkai' but tenkai means 'Turning' and there is a *tentai* kote hineri. This application is rather large in its preparatory actions but there are smaller, and more painful, variations.

14......Shiho Nage or Four Direction Throw. This will also be a familiar technique to Aikido devotees. It is surprising how many Tomiki-Style students, and Dan Grades, know and practise only the Kata application and are of the impression that Uke must always fall onto his back. The Uyeshiba and Shioda styles have some fine applications of this technique and one could do a lot worse than learn some of them.

UKI WAZA

Floating Techniques

15......Mae Otoshi or Forward Drop. In basic form this application is almost useless unless perfectly timed. Perhaps the timing usually being bad is the reason why it usually raises a guffaw or two from uninitiated onlookers. In variation form it is definitely more effective as the hip can be brought into play similarly to Judo's Uki Goshi.

16......Sumi Otoshi or Corner Drop. For the strong tall man who is not frightened to bend his knees this is a good application in either basic or variation form. Uke can be brought down either on his back, which can be painful, or by rolling backfall. Ukes are always advised to make the rolling breakfall as it is far safer.

17......Hiki Otoshi or Pull Drop. This is one technique which has undergone several changes, most of which are rarely effective due to bad timing or, in Kata form, a bad Uke. In variation form techniques are very similar to Judo's Osoto Maki Komi and Seio Otoshi fall into this category. Some schools shun such variations as being too dangerous...?

HOW SHOULD THE KATA BE DEMONSTRATED?

This should be an easy question to answer as the title of the Kata conveys the actual demonstration but over the years every Japanese instructor that has visited these shores has taught his own personal preference of this Kata and for many the real performance has been lost.

The Kata should represent a demonstration of randori!

The kata should be full of life and once both parties have commenced it should be non-stop up until the final application and submission by Uke. No stopping between sections to adjust gi, no stopping to correct bad applications or even if the sequence has been muddled. Both parties must work together with the same aim — to demonstrate. The demonstration should be kept as central to the demonstration area as possible. Both parties change positions during the Kata; one party does not remain at one end of the mat and the other party at the other. Even though changes of position are made both Uke and Tori must judge their ma-ai (distance) for each application to keep the demonstration neat and tidy. In competent hands the whole Kata should take about one minute.

The accompanying photographs have not been taken from one central position so as to try and convey as many of the major points as possible. Where a change of position is to be made it will be stated in the narrative. Every time Uke rises he makes his 'attack' from the position where he rises and does not move around to a prearranged spot with the speed and elegance of an elderly dowager suffering an arthritic attack! Regrettably our elderly dowager is symbolic of the manner in which this Kata is so frequently seen.

The matter of co-operation between Tori and Uke cannot be over emphasised. This is Kata — not a free-for-all. Kata should be the ultimate in co-operation between two persons. Perhaps this is why good Kata is so rarely seen — too much in our Martial and not enough in our Art? Both Tori and Uke must know their respective jobs and they must perform those duties. If Uke is bad then any amount of good work by Tori will not cover errors, and vice versa. Uke has to re-act according to the type of application being demonstrated and should comply with the application. Remember Aikido is the way of complying with, namely, an 'attacker' finds that his attack is used as a weapon against him. The technique should not 'work' regardless; it should comply with either the 'attack' or with Uke's re-actions!

Perhaps at this point I should interpose a personal opinion. This style of Aikido does employ deliberate breaking of balance. Namely, check attack, break balance, then apply the technique. I personally believe that such a principle is not Aikido; Aikido is to comply with not fight against. Though the reader will see the balance being broken referred to this is not meant to be taken as check, break balance then apply a technique but it is something incorporated in the application. In Aikido one's technique should be in harmony with the 'attack'. One should take advantage of bad or broken balance but one should not practise an application with the deliberate intention to break balance. If one does one goes against fundamental and basic principles of Aikido, regardless of style.

Applications should be smooth and with apparent snap and smartness. So many demonstrations of this Kata show both parties as being sad and depleted creatures without any pride or intent in their practice. Tori should keep good, though not rigid, posture. Uke should make his 'attacks' with apparent intent and not as though he is waving goodbye to his great aunt at a railway station. Posture for both parties can make a wealth of difference to those watching, apart from posture being one of the main, and overlooked, essentials of the practice of Aikido.

One cannot effect good practice if one remains rigid like a statue and not if one ambles around the mat like Quasimodo, and very many perform that way with considerable regularity.

Life, snap, smartness and confidence are the essentials of this Kata, plus knowledge and co-operation.

The demonstration should take about one minute, so what do we have to do in that minute? Quite a lot but first we have to judge our *ma-ai* or distance.

If Tori and Uke stand in a right basic posture with arms held at *Chudan* (central position) so that their hands touch, then resume, or retreat, into a neutral posture we have the correct ma-ai; *and that ma-ai must be the same for each application*, regardless of moving around or application. The distance has to be *judged* by Uke and not *set* as described above. Uke's attacks or moves to Tori should be in the form of an attempt to place the right cupped hand under Tori's chin (the type of application made by Tori in Shomen Ate) and this is done by Uke moving from neutral into a right basic posture, one step only. Of course, Uke's attack is way off target but Tori starts to move into the application immediately Uke starts his attack so the distance is never obvious. Apart from the fact that this is Kata and both parties should be demonstrating and one needs clear applications this is supposed to represent a one-sided display of randori. In randori one would not allow the opponent to get to within attacking range but take advantage immediately an arm was 'presented'. This must be conveyed in the Kata – Tori seizing upon opportunity.

So, our ma-ai has been set, we bow, and now we start.

Hand and Arm positions referred to in the narrative.

Jodan

Chudan

Gedan

The *Chudan* position is the *Basic Posture* position.

Judging Correct Ma-ai

Correct Ma-ai

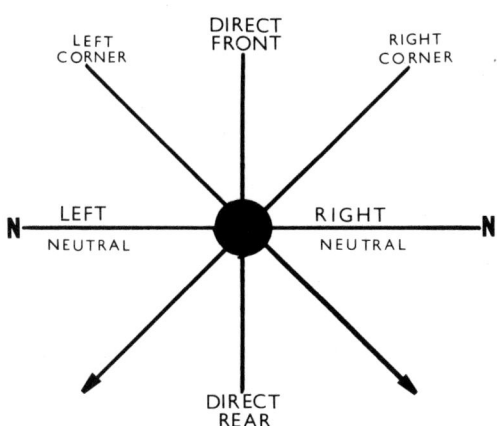
Directions referred to in the text.

ATEMI WAZA

ATEMI WAZA ....SUMMARY OF UKE'S REACTIONS

1. Shomen Ate........As attacking arm is removed a slight loss of upper-body balance is lost forwards; regain to full posture.

2. Ai Gamae Ate.......Loss of balance on check to elbow towards rear left.

3. Gyaku Gamae Ate...Loss of balance of upper-body forwards; regain full posture.

4. Gedan Ate.........Loss of balance to direct rear as attack is made to head — no loss forwards on initial check.

5. Ushiro Ate.........Loss of balance towards rear left; movement of right leg to left neutral necessary to maintain balance.

ATEMI WAZA

1. Shomen Ate — Chin (Front Head) Attack

Tori	Uke
	Make Attack.
Immediately attack is started move from neutral towards right front corner (one small step only), raising right arm to Jodan (high) position, and taking left leg into right posture — right foot pointing directly between Uke's feet. Bring right handblade down onto Uke's arm midway between wrist and elbow and remove attacking arm down to own hip level. Place left handblade onto Uke's right wrist; take right hand across body to centre, cup the hand and move straight up Uke's chest 'attacking' his chin. As contact is made drive head back and push firmly with *both* hands, right under chin and left against wrist, making tsugi-ashi between Uke's legs.	Allow head to be driven back. Arch back, stagger to rear and fall onto back.
Hold right basic posture for a count of '2' then retreat into neutral posture.	Rise and move in for next attack.

NOTES: Tori should make attack smoothly but firm. Do not push with shoulders but with whole body. The 'steps' are not actual steps but the feet are *slid* forwards in tsugi-ashi, not *steps*.

Shomen Ate

ATEMI WAZA

2. Ai Gamae Ate — Regular Posture Attack

Tori	Uke
Step into right posture, deflect attack with back of right hand then immediately step into left posture, taking left hand to gripping Uke's elbow, thumb below and fingers uppermost, making a firm push with that left hand towards Uke's left shoulder.	Make attack. Allow balance to be disturbed to rear left corner.
Remove right hand in large movement and bring up from under Uke's right arm into cupping position under chin. The right hand *must* now be kept in the centre of your body. Drive Uke's head to his rear and across to his rear right corner.	Balance now disturbed to rear right corner.
As hand is moved to Uke's rear right turn body, maintaining right hand in centre of body, and bring right leg through. Make tsugi-ashi.	Take right leg back in attempt to maintain balance. Stagger back and fall.
Hold right basic posture for count of '2' then retreat into neutral.	Rise, move in for next attack.

NOTES: The technique is not applied by forcing Uke straight back but by disturbing balance to rear left and right respectively. Tori holds Uke's right arm at Chudan throughout the application until Uke starts to fall, then releases hold on elbow.

Ai Gamae Ate

ATEMI WAZA

3. Gyaku Gamae Ate — Reverse Posture Attack

Tori	Uke
	Make attack.
Step into right posture, placing right hand on top of Uke's right forearm and remove attacking arm from chudan to gedan, at centre of body.	Initial removing of arm causes slight loss of balance to front; lose posture then regain to upright position.
As Uke's head rises to full posture bring left hand across body to right hip, hand open and fingers extended. As Uke reaches full posture drive left hand thumb-edge towards Uke's forehead and change position of the hand so that little-finger edge makes vertical contact with the forehead. Left hand is now the attacking hand and the left leg must move in co-ordination with the left arm. Drive head back and make tsugi-ashi.	Make as though head is being driven back, arch back and fall.
Release right hand hold on forearm. Hold left basic posture for '2' then retreat into neutral.	Rise and move in for next attack.

NOTES: Attack to head should be smooth but firm. Contact with forehead is made as Uke regains full posture. Hand should be *vertical* — the horizontal palm application is made when there is no control on the arm.

Gyaku Gamae Ate

ATEMI WAZA

4. Gedan Ate — Low Position Attack

Tori	Uke
	Make attack.
Step into right posture, remove arm, attack with left hand and step into left posture exactly as with the previous application.	Initial move does not break balance as you are prepared for the possible application of gyaku gamae ate. As attack comes to forehead raise both arms to check, making check with left hand forearm.
As Uke tries to defend remove left hand from attacking commitment and turn whole body to the right, so that you are facing right in a neutral posture. Take left arm under Uke's right arm and follow with whole body. Uke's right arm being held across the shoulders. Place left arm against Uke's thighs, arm slightly bowed. Turn hard left into left posture and make hard tsugi-ashi.	Remain in upright posture. Balance lost to rear, stagger and fall onto back.
Do not 'step' straight forward but towards own left front corner. Hold left Gedan posture for '2' then resume neutral.	Rise and move in for next attack.

NOTES: The finalisation of the application is brought about by the hard body turn and not by a straight push. The step to the left front corner is made to avoid Uke falling across the leg and disturbs the balance that much extra.

Gedan Ate

ATEMI WAZA

5. Ushiro Ate — Rear Attack

Tori	Uke
	Make attack.
Step into right posture, deflect attack with back of right hand and with the *palm* of the left hand — Right hand to wrist and left at elbow. Drive with both hands towards Uke's rear left corner. This 'drive' is started from the centre position, down to a low position and up to a high position; it is best described as a dipping action.	Drive to rear corner causes loss of balance — counteract loss by turning whole body 180 degrees to rear into neutral position.
As Uke's turn is beginning step forward on left to own left front corner level with Uke, ending in neutral posture. Place right hand on Uke's right shoulder and left upon left. Step back strongly on *left* leg into right posture and make tsugi-ashi to own rear. Hold posture until Uke falls then turn into neutral posture.	Stagger back and fall. Rise and move in for next attack.

The first change of positions has been made.

NOTES: The check, drive, spin and move by Tori should all be done simultaneously, thereby applying the 'attack' before Uke can regain his full balance. Uke should be drawn back so that he falls behind Tori, who can also finalise the application by kneeling on the left knee.

Ushiro Ate

HIJI WAZA

HIJI WAZA .... SUMMARY OF UKE'S REACTIONS

6. Oshi Taoshi......... Loss of balance towards right front; sliding of right leg forward necessary to maintain balance.

7. Ude Gaeshi......... Resist attempt to break balance as done in Oshi Taoshi and lower elbow to prevent attempt to Push Down.

8. Hiki Taoshi......... Balance of upper-body broken forward and moving of left leg to neutral necessary to prevent loss to front right.

9. Ude Hineri .... Resist attempt to break as for Hiki Taoshi; remain in right posture and pull back right arm.

10. Waki Gatame ...... Attack made with strong arm, attempt to counter any of the previous Hiji applications.

HIJI WAZA

6. Oshi Taoshi — Push Down

Tori	Uke
	Make attack.
Step into right posture, check outside attacking arm with right handblade at wrist and with left hand gripping forearm, fingers uppermost. Grip with right hand and make small tsugi-ashi to own rear left corner, drawing Uke and 'working' the arm so that his elbow is higher than the hand.	Balance is broken to front right, counteract this by sliding right foot forward.
Immediately Uke moves to try and regain balance slide left hand up to the elbow joint and firmly drive that hand towards Uke's head, take left leg forward and bring that left hand, holding the elbow, down to the inside of the left thigh.	Turn body left and prepare to go down onto stomach. Go onto stomach.
Take right leg forward, left leg placed near Uke's right armpit and the held right wrist under your right knee. Ensure Uke's arm is being held at more than a 90 degree angle from his body (make tsugi-ashi to correct if necessary). Apply gentle pressure against elbow joint.	Submit.
Release hold and move *forward* into neutral posture, facing Uke.	Rise and move in for next attack.

Second change of position has been made.

NOTES: Initial attack to the elbow should be firm and smooth and should be timed to catch Uke off balance.

Oshi Taoshi

HIJI WAZA

7. Ude Gaeshi — Arm Turn

Tori	Uke
	Make attack.
Step into right posture, check outside and make initial actions exactly as for the previous technique.	
	If Tori succeeds in breaking your balance and raising the elbow Oshi Taoshi can be applied — resist attempt to break balance and make definite move to keep elbow low.
As resistance is felt step forward on left leg releasing hold with left hand, turn body so that you are at right angles to Uke and in a neutral posture and right hand is at the centre of your body. Entangle Uke's arm and turn body to left, into left posture, and drive the left entangled arm over Uke's right shoulder making tsugi-ashi.	
	Allow arm to be turned back, arch back, stagger and fall.
As Uke begins to fall release hold. Hold left posture for '2' then resume neutral.	Rise and move in for next attack.

NOTES: It is Tori's left hand that does the work — leave that hand open as no power is gained from the clenched fist — keep Uke's right arm folded as close to his head as possible. In variation form the arm can be turned away from the head but not in Kata.

Ude Gaeshi

HIJI WAZA

8. Hiki Taoshi — Pull Down

Tori	Uke
	Make attack.
Step into right posture, check outside the attacking arm with the right handblade, grip with that right hand and bring the left hand into play. Grip the forearm with the left hand, fingers lower and thumb uppermost (the opposite grip to that of Oshi Taoshi). Take Uke's right arm out towards own right shoulder then, making tsugi-ashi to your rear draw both hands down to your stomach, moving midway between direct rear a rear left corner.	The taking of the attacking arm out to your left and the drawing forward causes loss of balance, counteract by taking left leg forward into a neutral posture.
Uke's balance is now weakest towards his direct front. Release right hand grip, raise that right hand to Jodan, maintain tsugi-ashi and bring the right hand down onto Uke's elbow joint, placing the thumb on the inside of Uke's arm. Apply pressure against joint.	As balance goes forward go down onto stomach.
Immediately Uke is on the floor hold wrist beneath right knee and increase pressure against joint.	Submit.
Release hold and retreat to neutral	Rise and move in for next attack.

NOTES: Initial breaking of balance should be firm but smooth. Immediately this move has been made Tori should make his rear tsugi-ashi and keep doing so until Uke is on the floor.

Hiki Taoshi

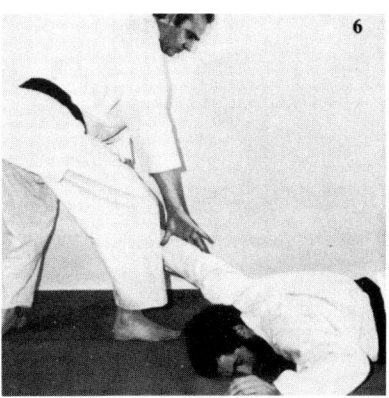

HIJI WAZA

9. Ude Hineri — Arm Twist

Tori	Uke
	Make attack.
Step into right posture make attempt previous technique — Hiki Taoshi.	Remembering the previous application resist attempt to break balance. Allow arm to be taken from Chudan to Gedan but resist attempt to break balance.
As resistance to pull is felt release right hand hold and step forward on left to position directly level with Uke's right foot. As step to Uke's rear is made take his right arm up his back into a *back-hammer* position.	Assume a crouched position as arm is turned up the back.
Take right arm over Uke's upper arm and under the forearm placing the palm against own left forearm. Face direct front and make tentai, turning to own right 180 degrees, keeping both feet in firm contact with the mat. Lever against Uke's shoulder joint.	As pressure is felt against the shoulder take left leg forward and make a left hand rolling breakfall.
Release hold as Uke goes into a roll and hold right posture for '2'. Advance left into neutral.	Rise immediately. Move in for next attack.

Third change of position has been made.

NOTES: When moving in on left leg anchor right foot firmly.

Ude Hineri

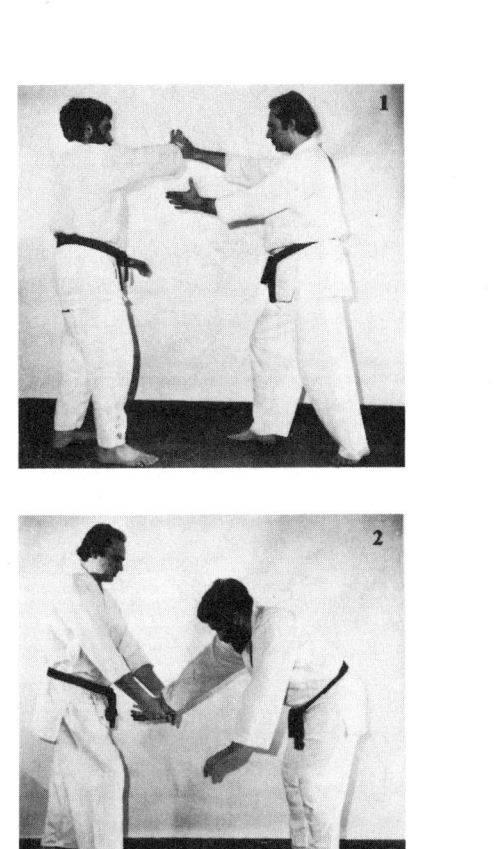

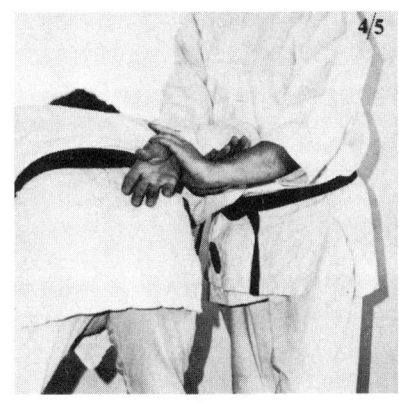
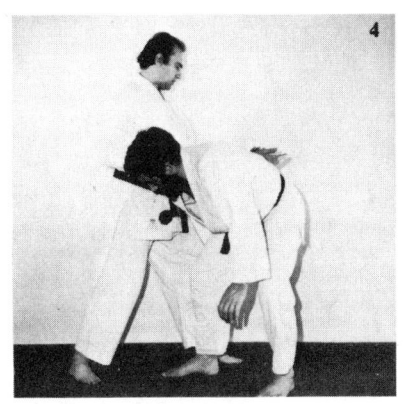

HIJI WAZA

10. Waki Gatame — Side Lock.

Tori	Uke
	Make attack.
Step into right posture and check with left hand gripping forearm — fingers uppermost — and with right hand held palm up with the thumb of the left hand against the palm. Grip only with left hand and wrap right hand fingers around own left hand fingers — hold at Chudan and start tsugi-ashi between direct front and right front corner. Start to turn Uke's arm by using the left hand as though operating the throttle of a motor-cycle turning the arm so that the palm of that right hand is uppermost and using the forearm of your left hand as a bar to aid the turning of the arm.	Do not resist tsugi-ashi.
	Make tentai to your left as tsugi-ashi is applied.
Left arm should slide over Uke's right arm so that Uke's tricep is under your armpit. Slide right hand under Uke's arm and trap the wrist into the elbow crook and draw firmly to the chest, as low down as possible. Take right leg across and turn left into neutral and apply pressure against the elbow joint.	As Tori turns at right angles slide right leg behind Tori for balance. Submit to pressure against joint.
Release hold and take left leg back into neutral, facing Uke.	Move in for next attack.

Fourth change of position has been made

NOTES: Tori should keep arms at Chudan until leverage is applied. Uke should remain upright until leverage is applied then *maintain balance*.

Waki Gatame

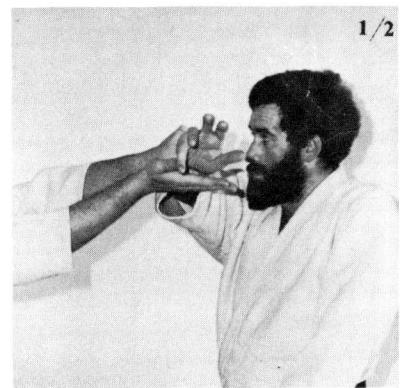

TEKUBI WAZA

TEKUBI WAZA ...... SUMMARY OF UKE'S REACTIONS.

11. Kote Hineri .... Attack as for Waki Gatame, strong arm. Use of wrist/forearm joint break balance to front right and sliding of right leg forward necessary to maintain balance.

12. Kote Gaeshi ...... Resist attempt to apply Kote Hineri and, as for Ude Gaeshi, resist by lowering elbow.

13. Tenkai Kote Hineri. Slight resistance towards rear left corner, and drawing of right arm back towards rear right.

14. Shiho Nage .... Upper-body balance broken towards front right, attempt to regain full posture.

TEKUBI WAZA

11. Kote Hineri — Forearm Twist

Tori	Uke
	Make attack.
Step into right posture gripping forearm with left hand, fingers uppermost, and with right hand lightly grip Uke's fingers taking hold with own thumb underneath against lower finger joints. Make tsugi-ashi towards own rear left corner, as for Oshi Taoshi, and begin to twist Uke's wrist so the palm of the hand is towards you and break the balance.	Attempt to regain balance by sliding the right foot forward, as for Oshi Taoshi.
Immediately Uke tries to regain balance slide left hand up to elbow and push as for Oshi Taoshi but maintain, and continue, twist on wrist/forearm. Take left leg through, momentary control, then into right posture releasing left hand hold on elbow. Maintain twist, hold own right elbow firmly into your right hip, place left leg against Uke's right hip and increase twist. Release hold and retreat into neutral posture.	Make tentai. Go down onto stomach. Submit. Rise and move in for next attack.

NOTES: Initial check and grips should be made simultaneously. Do not grip Uke's fingers too hard and maintain twist throughout application.

Kote Hineri

TEKUBI WAZA

12. Kote Gaeshi — Forearm Turn

Tori	Uke
	Make attack.
Step, check, grip and step to own rear left corner exactly as for Kote Hineri.	As attempt to break balance is made resist. Do not try to draw held arm back but attempt, as with Ude Gaeshi, to lower elbow.
As resistance is felt step out on right to point midway between right front corner and right neutral then take left leg into right posture. As these steps are made turn Uke's forearm/wrist so that the back of the hand is towards you and slide left hand into kote-gaeshi-grip, fingers gripping palm below thumb and own left thumb against thumb-forefinger fork. Release right hand grip and take kote-gaeshi-grip with the right hand, thumb against third-finger knuckle and fingers against palm. Now firmly turn the forearm/wrist towards your left hip. As Uke goes into rolling breakfall anchor right foot and take left leg back behind you into right posture and retain hold on wrist. Strong posture. As Uke hits the ground hold position for '2', release hold and retreat into neutral.	Do not resist attempt to stretch arm and do not move forward. Rise onto toes and prepare for *rolling breakfall*. Into roll. Rise and move in for next attack.

Fifth change of position has been made.

NOTES: When turning the wrist/forearm Tori should press with the thumbs and pull with the fingers in an anti-clockwise direction. When Uke makes his breakfall he should throw his head over the right arm and between his feet — *not jump over the arm.*

Kote Gaeshi

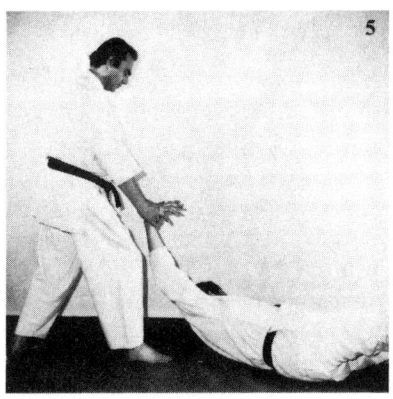

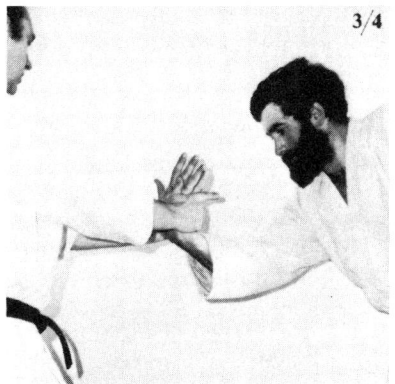

TEKUBI WAZA

13. Tenkai Kote Hineri – Turning Forearm Twist.

Tori	Uke
Step into right posture, check outside with right handblade. Grip forearm with right just above wrist joint, taking the hand slightly out to the right then back across the body to the left, at shoulder height. As the hand reaches the centre of your body bring the left hand into play, grip Uke's wrist with left thumb against back of the hand and fingers against palm, release right hand grip and slide that hand up to the elbow. As move reaches your left step forward on the left leg and with the right hand at the elbow break Uke's balance to his rear right corner.	Make attack.
	Allow balance to be broken.
Both hands at just above Chudan, take right leg through, take both hands back and as they reach directly above your head make tentai, turning into left posture. Release right hand hold and apply twist with left hand.	
	Rise onto toes as twist is applied.
Hold left hand grip at centre of body at Chudan.	
Raise right hand to Jodan and draw left hand down to Gedan, keeping strong twist. Slide right leg forward and turn, facing Uke, into right posture. Bring right hand from Jodan down onto Uke's right arm at the elbow, placing palm against elbow joint with thumb on the inside of the arm.	Bend from hips, forwards to your right front corner.
	Prepare to go down onto stomach.
Maintain twist, apply leverage against elbow joint and make tsugi-ashi to your direct rear. In a right posture, place your left gripping-hand on the inside of your right leg just below the knee, place the right hand on the elbow joint (no leverage against the joint) and increase the twist with the left hand.	Go down onto stomach.
	Submit.
Release hold and retreat into neutral.	Rise and move in for next attack.

NOTES: Immediately Uke's balance is broken to his rear right corner the right leg of Tori has to be taken through and a fast tentai made. The twist on the wrist/forearm has to be maintained throughout the application and the removal of the left hand from Chudan to very low Gedan has to be strong.

Tenkai Kote Hineri

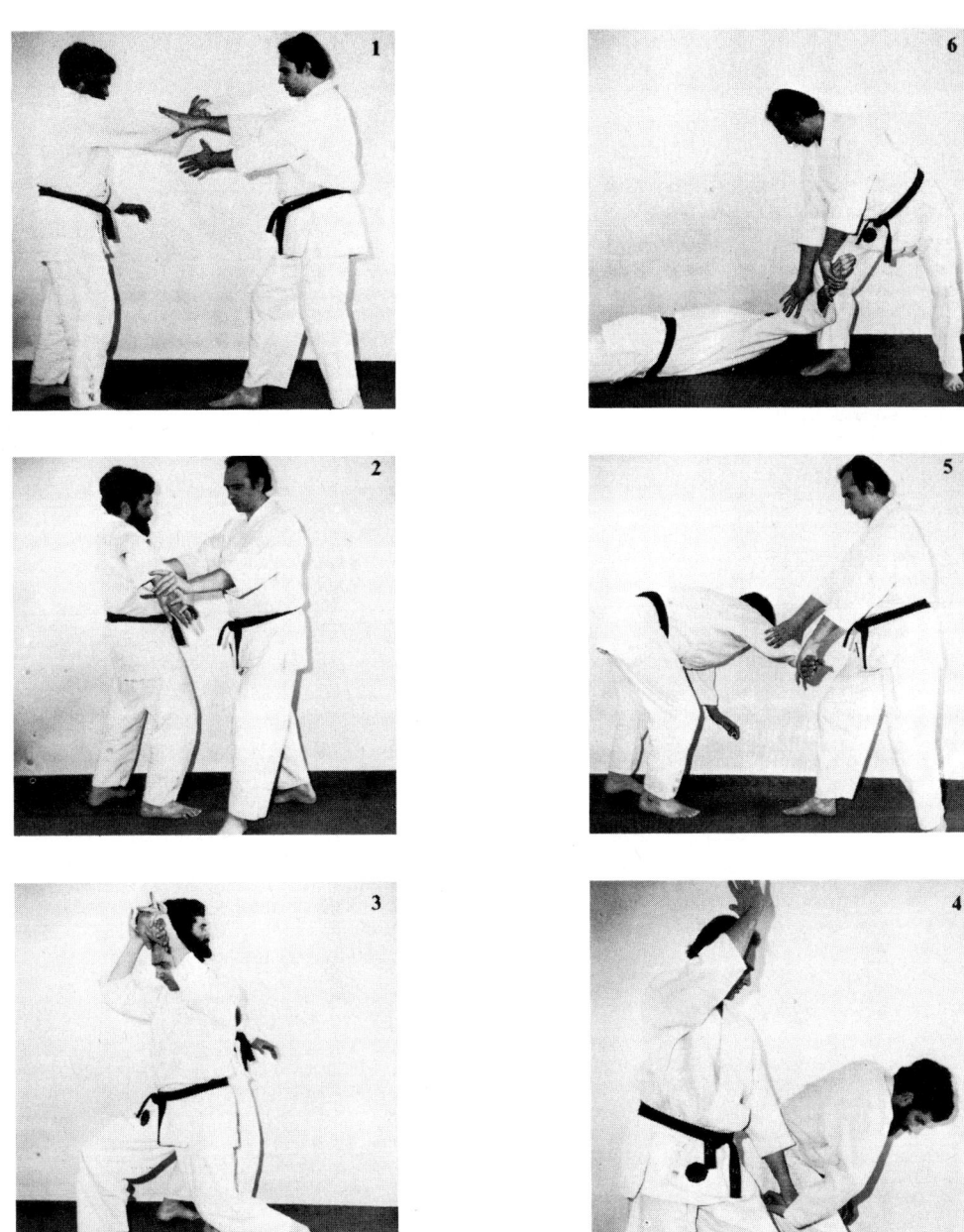

TEKUBI WAZA

14. Shiho Nage — Four Direction Throw.

Tori	Uke
	Make attack.
Step into right posture and 'check' with both hands; right hand from beneath with the palm uppermost and the left hand from inside with the handblade. Gripping with the right hand remove Uke's arm from Chudan, down to midway between Gedan and Chudan then up to Chudan, as this is done step with the right foot out to your right just above neutral position. As you complete this step and the arm removal grip with the left hand, thumb uppermost, and apply our motor-cycle-throttle action with the right hand.	Allow balance to be broken, bend from hips to your front but you should be partially facing your left front corner.
Facing almost your right neutral in a right posture, take your left foot and place it beside your right into a neutral posture. Take the right leg back into a left posture, raising both hands as though taking both over your head; as both hands reach directly above your head make tentai, turning into a right posture. Straighten right arm and release left grip.	Allow arm to be folded back.
Make tsugi-ashi, pressing downwards with the right hand.	Arch back, stagger and fall.
As Uke starts to fall release hold. Hold Chudan for '2'. Retreat into neutral.	Rise and move in for next attack.

NOTES: When retreating on the right leg from neutral and making tentai into right posture the turn should be made fast. On making tsugi-ashi the right hand holding Uke's forearm/wrist, must be driven downwards. It is usually good practice for Tori to aim that right hand for a spot that is about Uke's height on the mat to his rear.

Shiho Nage

UKI WAZA

UKI WAZA . . . . SUMMARY OF UKE'S REACTIONS

15. Mae Otoshi. . . . . . . .Upper-body balance broken slightly as for Shiho Nage but expecting Shiho application resist towards rear left.

16. Sumi Otoshi. . . . . . .Initial taking of right arm implies either application of Shiho or Mae Otoshi, resist both towards rear right.

17. Hiki Otoshi. . . . . . . .As attack is made Tori moves out fo range but too late for Uke to adjust. Reach for Tori and lose balance forwards.

UKI WAZA

15. Mae Otoshi — Forward Drop.

Tori	Uke

Uke: Make attack.

Tori: Step into right posture, check and grip as for Shiho Nage. Remove arm from Chudan to midway between Chudan and own hips, making a small step to a position between own direct front and front right corner.

Uke: From right posture make a quarter turn to your left into neutral posture.

Tori: Place left hand palm against Uke's right tricep. Start to step through onto left foot (into left posture) and as you do so start to turn the left arm from a palm-uppermost state through a 270 degree turn (clockwise) and raise your right holding hand to Chudan. Intend to 'hit' Uke's tricep with your own upper left arm, very lightly lowering the elbow joint.

Uke: As leverage is felt against elbow, rise onto your toes and from a neutral position (facing Tori's direct right) prepare for a rolling breakfall on the left.

Tori: As contact with your upper arm and Uke's tricep is made make strong tsugi-ashi to your direct front. As Uke starts to fall release hold and maintain left posture at Chudan for '2'. Then move into neutral.

Uke: Make rolling breakfall.

Rise and move in for next attack.

NOTES: Tori's step through must be accompanied with a strong 'screwing' action with the left arm. Uke, the correct fall *must* be made.

Mae Otoshi

UKI WAZA

16. Sumi Otoshi — Corner Drop.

Tori	Uke
	Make attack.
Step in on right leg, check and grip exactly as for Shiho Nage and Mae Otoshi at Chudan. Take arm from right across body to left Chudan, releasing right hand grip as you do so and sliding that right hand up to Uke's elbow joint, thumb towards you, step into left deep posture and drive upwards with both hands, towards Uke's rear right corner.	Remain in right posture and allow balance to be broken to rear right corner.
Drive firmly out towards your front left corner with the right hand at the elbow joint.	From a *right posture*, turn upper body to your right, turning to your rear right corner, and go into a right rolling breakfall.
Bring left hand down to inside of left knee. Keep strong posture and retain holds. After Uke falls hold position for '2', release holds and retreat into neutral.	Rise and move in for next attack.

NOTES: Tori on stepping forwards on the left leg must raise both arms strongly upwards and out to his front left corner. As with the previous application, Uke must make the correct fall, and that is not stepping back on the right leg for his roll; he remains in right posture facing Tori's rear and goes into the roll from *that* position.

Sumi Otoshi

UKI WAZA

17. Hiki Otoshi — Pull Drop

Tori	Uke
	Make attack, not the usual 'pulled' attack but as though lunging for the target.
As attack is mounted make small step on right towards own right front corner and take left leg into right posture. Check inside attacking arm with both hands — left to wrist with handblade then grip; right to elbow with thumb uppermost and fingers under elbow joint, then grip. Turn the left hand grip so that the back of your hand turns uppermost. Make a strong tentai to your left keeping both hands as near central to your body as possible and start to apply leverage against the elbow joint. Now draw both hands strongly from Chudan to lowest Gedan.	Start to completely lose balance to your direct front. Make rolling breakfall, on right.
As Uke starts to go into the roll keep right leg firm and take left leg back into right posture. As Uke hits the ground slide right hand so that palm is against the back of the elbow joint and apply lock.	
Release hold and retreat to neutral.	Submit. Rise and face Tori in neutral.

Final change in position has been made.
Both parties should be in the *same positions* on the *same spots* as at the start.
Adjust Gi ... Rei.

NOTES: Uke's correct actions either make or break this application. Uke's attack must be a lunge, if not this is a 'nothing' technique in Kata form.

Hiki Otoshi

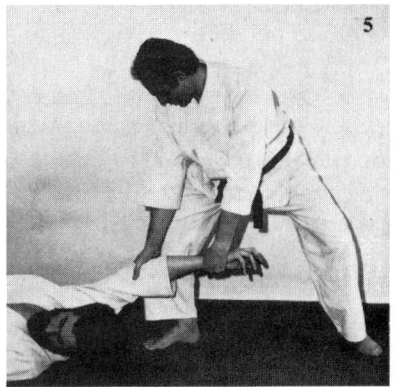

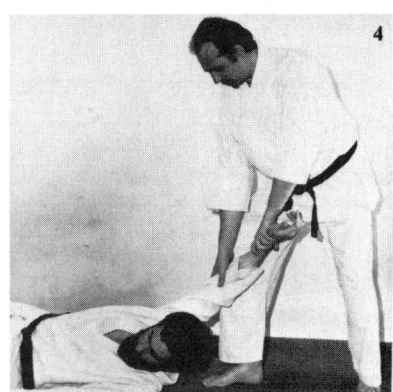

VARIATIONS

The Tomiki-Style is one that undergoes frequent change. Whether such changes are for the better or worse is something that is open to much speculation. Over the past fourteen years I have never come across any Japanese instructor who has taught Randori-No-Kata the same way as one of his predecessors. "It's been changed," used to be a catch phrase in this style of Aikido, in fact in some quarters it still is. I personally believe that the changes in teaching by visiting Japanese have been brought about because when in the UK they are far removed from their seniors at Waseda and they can teach what they want to teach instead of what they should teach. One cannot progress in either ability or in knowledge if one can only learn for a limited period before the whole lot is changed again.

The right and wrong ways are matters that are under frequent fire in Aikido. Someone once told me that the right way is the way that works — perhaps there is considerable truth in that.

I have found that what is a good application on one person is perfectly useless on another. Allowance for varying size and build etc. are allowances rarely made by the 'must' people. Any Budoka will realise that in free-style there is a great deal of room for variation; and yet, in this style there are still those who insist that this foot *must* be put here — no, two inches further left — and that arm *must* be held there — no, two and one-third degrees higher. Variation over basic is one thing that, for the best part, remains a Shangri-La world.

There is no reason why, retaining the traditions of Kata and basic points, we should not vary our free-practice. There is no reason why *we* should not use our natural strengths. There is no reason why *we* should not have a little more 'spice' in our free-practice, providing both parties agree to it. And still allow and encourage the practice of movement.

In the following Variation Section there may well be some applications that many Aikidoka will frown in horror upon. In some dojos of this style to apply some of them would result in banishment to distant parts yet there is not one variation included that is not applied with considerable frequency in my dojo. Of course, application is relevant to the ability and the knowledge of the person one is practising with. Some applications may be 'too near Judo' for some but where does one draw the definition line between a Judo application and an Aikido application? Perhaps such realisation is like beauty and lies in the eyes of the beholder but it would take a naive person to draw a definite line. To many of us there are close links between Aikido, Judo and even Karate, but to many others they are three poles apart. Aikido and Judo had the same mother, father and were almost delivered by the same midwife — *Jujitsu*. So, why not include a little basic Judo in our free-practice? Perhaps we have to use our own conclusions about where we should draw the line between acceptable and prohibitive applications.

In the following pages there is one variation for each of the preceding Kata applications. The student of this style who has a reasonable working-knowledge of the Kata should be able to adapt them with, I hope reasonable ease and fluency. As with the Kata plates the photographs have not been taken from one angle but from varying points so as to try and convey as much as possible. The narrative is not as lengthy as the Kata and in places might be regarded as rather abrupt. In variations there can be no hard and fast rules. What to one person is an easy and effective application will be ineffective to another. One has to adapt and as far as variations are concerned the individual has to adapt to him or her self and their particular style. If we look at our style of variation on Gedan Ate; I have one student who catches opponents with this virtually every time he tries it — others find it an awkward application.

There is, of course, more than one variation for each technique but it is hoped that, apart from making free-practice a little less mundane, it might make some students of the style think of and work out their own variations, particularly the students of *basic-randori*.

To those who are unfamiliar with the variations shown here a word of caution is given. Throughout the application the welfare of your Uke should be foremost in your mind. In free-practice, whether it be randori or ka kari geiko, apply techniques commensurate with Uke's grade. Do not underestimate any of these applications; they look harmless, they are not. Many can be applied with very hard force! This is where narrative and photographs serve only to enlighten. There is no substitute for competent instruction.

Throughout these applications Uke's attack should be with the cupped-hand and directly at Tori's chin — not pulled one pace away as the Kata technqiues are. When practising these Uke is advised to keep relaxed and go with any application. Apart from the fact that when one is trying to practise a 'wise-guy' Uke is very patience-trying, Tori just might catch Uke with everything *right*, if Uke is stiff and resisting he just might go down and find it extremely difficult when he tries to get up.

As with the Kata, practice right and left side applications, start slowly then build up to fast attack and fast applications.

1 .... Shomen Ate .... Variation — Shomen Ate-Osoto Gake.

Tori is best advised to assume a left posture, Uke will attack with the right hand.

As the attack is made, turn your body to the right and avoid the attack. Make fast tsugi-ashi, taking the left arm around Uke's left hip and the right up to attack the chin. Now, drive the right hand back and draw the left hand and Uke's body towards you. With the left leg hook Uke's right leg just below the knee and try drawing that left leg back towards you as though you intend to end in a right posture. Release left hand from the back as Uke starts to fall.

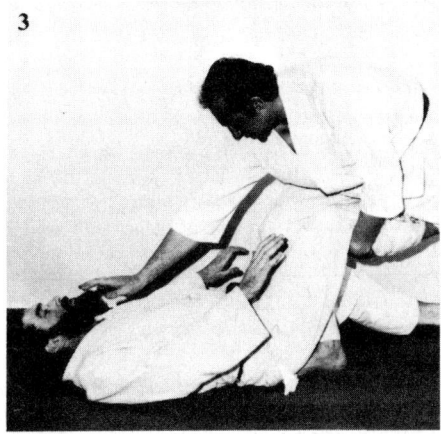

2........ Ai Gamae Ate .... Variation – Irimi Nage

Assume left posture. Avoid attacking hand by inclining upper body to your left. Bring up left hand and with the palm 'strike' the elbow, firmly. Bring up the right hand, under Uke's right arm and turn that hand so that the back is facing you, thumb downwards. Take the right leg through into a right posture driving the right hand towards Uke's left shoulder, over that shoulder and to the back of his head. Now, drive that right hand, fingers extended, downwards and towards Uke's direct rear.

3......... Gyaku Gamae Ate .... Variation — Gyaku Gamae Ate/Obi Otoshi

Assume left posture. As attack is made incline head to your left and bring the left arm up, over and down onto the attacking arm. When using that left arm extend the fingers and as it is brought down onto the arm turn the hand so that the thumb is pointing downwards. Take the right arm over Uke's right arm and grip the belt (or cloth around the belt knot area) and turning the left hand so that the palm is uppermost attack Uke's throat. Before application is made turn the hand so that the little-finger edge comes into contact with the underneath of Uke's chin. Now, pull out towards your right with the right hand grip and push to your left with the left handblade under Uke's chin. Turn left and make tsugi-ashi forwards.

4. . . . . Gedan Ate . . . . Variation — Gedan Ate-Ushiro Gake

Assume right posture. As attack is made lower hips and turn right under the attacking arm. Place the right hand behind Uke's right thigh and extend the left hand as you do for Kata Gedan Ate. Take the left leg forward and place it behind Tori, hooking just below the knees. Keep the left hand firm and sacrifice yourself pulling Uke's right leg as you fall.

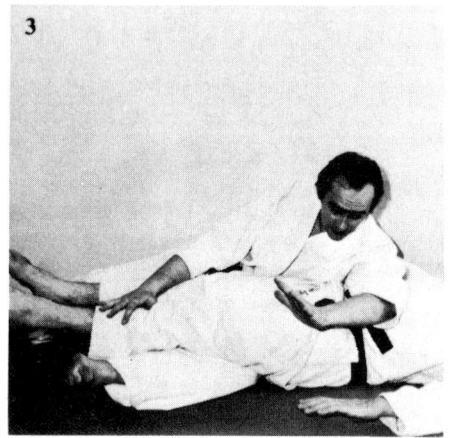

5 . . . . Ushiro Ate . . . . Variation — Ushiro Ate

Assume right posture, check (better as a deflection) the attacking arm with the back of the right hand. Step forward, deeply, on the left as near to Uke's left rear corner as possible. This is best attempted as a 'leap' as it adds considerable momentum to the application. Place the right hand in the small of Uke's back and take the thumb-edge of the left hand under Uke's chin. Go down into a kneeling position — either knee uppermost — push with the right hand and pull back with the left.

6......... Oshi Taoshi......... Variation — Oshi Taoshi

Assume right posture. As attack is made bring up right arm, checking under the attacking arm with the right forearm as near to own and Uke's wrists as possible. Bring left hand in and firmly attack Uke's elbow, making contact with fingers uppermost and thumb beneath, now drive hard with that left hand *directly for Uke's face*. Grip the wrist with your right hand, take the right leg forward and kneel with the left knee onto Uke's back as near to the centre of the back as possible. Now, lever against the elbow joint.

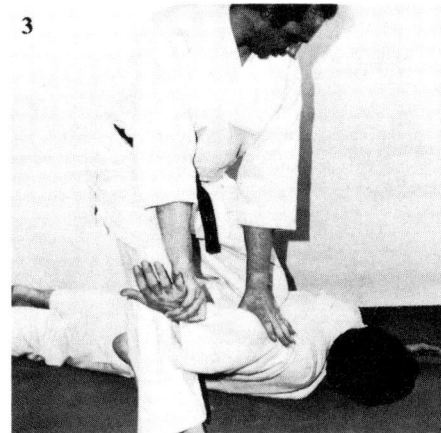

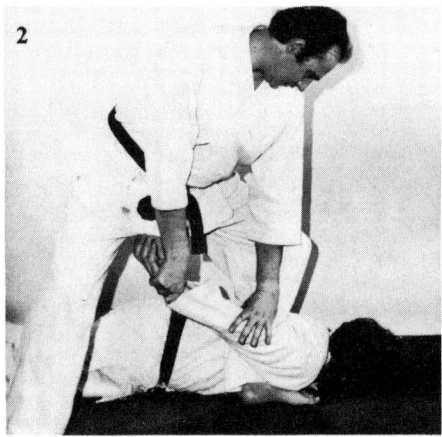

7........ Ude Gaeshi .... Variation – Ude Gaeshi

Assume right posture and check outside with right handblade, grip wrist and take left leg forward turning to a right neutral. As you turn to that position take the left arm over Uke's right forearm and then take your left hand beneath Uke's arm with the fingers extended. Now, turn hard left and gently take Uke's folded-back arm slightly away from his shoulder, turning your own body to the left as you do so, use your right foot as a pivot and retreat in anti-clockwise direction, driving continually forwards with your left handblade.

8......... Hiki Taoshi .... Variation — Hiki Taoshi

Assume right posture. As attack is made make tsugi-ashi to your direct rear, bring up right hand, check underneath attacking arm with handblade then grip Uke's forearm above the wrist; with the left hand palm uppermost take grip on forearm just below your right hand grip. Now strongly draw both hands downwards between your own retreating feet; 'walk' backwards, bearing firmly down all the time turning your grips in a clockwise direction. When Uke is on the ground kneel with the right knee directly between the shoulder blades, reverse your right hand grip and draw Uke's arm towards your right hip.

9. . . . . Ude Hineri . . . . Variation — Ude Hineri or Kata Gatame

Assume left posture and as attack is made make small tsugi-ashi to your direct rear, bringing up left hand, palm uppermost, and grip Uke's forearm. Now, step deep on the left and turn Uke's arm up his back into the back-hammer position. Take your right arm over Uke's upper arm and under the forearm, laying the palm of your right hand against your left forearm. Draw both hands close to your chest, turn in a clockwise direction levering Uke's shoulder and lowering your weight onto him. When Uke is on the floor continue the leverage of the shoulder until submission is given.

10. . . . . Waki Gatame . . . . Variation — Waki Gatame

Assume left posture. As attack is made turn slightly to your right and lean your head back to avoid attack. Bring up left arm over Uke's attacking arm taking care to avoid armpit contact with the elbow, bring up right arm to a near Jodan position and trap Uke's wrist in the crook of your right arm. Draw right forearm back past your right ear, trap wrist and now lower your right elbow towards your right hip. Incline a little weight onto the arm with your left arm and make strong *Hasso Unsuku* (sideways foot movements) to your right, lowering weight onto the arm as you do so until Uke submits.

11........ Kote Hineri .... Variation — Kote Hineri

Assume right posture and check/grip exactly as for Kata Kote Hineri. Either practise from an attack or, better still, practise from Uke offering a hand with fingers in basic posture position. Start to apply twist then release grip on Uke's fingers and using the palm of your right hand push Uke's fingers up towards his elbow or armpit.

12........ Kote Gaeshi .... Variation – Kote Gaeshi

Assume right posture (or left), as attack is make step to your left and check with right handblade, grip forearm and then bring the left hand across to take Kote-Gaeshi grip. Release right hand grip and take Kote Gaeshi grip with that. Now, if in left posture take left leg back and around in an anti-clockwise move so that you end in a right posture facing Uke's right neutral. If in right posture make small step to your own right neutral and take the left leg back so that you end in a right posture as described. Start to apply turn with left hand, release grip with right fingers and placing the palm of the right hand against the back of Uke's hand apply a turn with your right hand in a sharp anti-clockwise direction – namely in the direction of your own left hip. Uke may well be taken down onto his knees and then will be forced to turn onto his back.

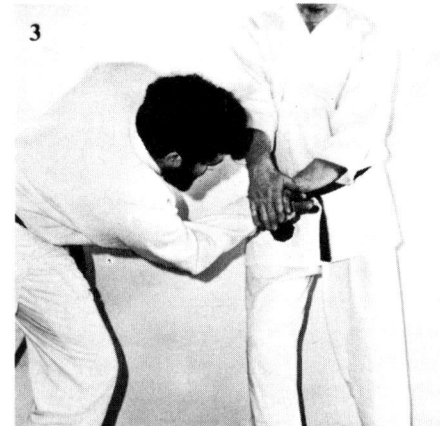

13........ Tenkai Kote Hineri .... Variation – Tentai Kote Hineri

Assume right posture. Check attack as for Kata Tenkai Kote Hineri. Do not attempt to break balance as in Kata but having secured your grip pull Uke directly on to you, as he comes forward slide the right leg a little further forward and with the right hand firmly gripping his forearm take that arm over your head, make a very fast tentai, apply strong Gyaku Hineri and 'walk' to your direct rear, bearing down on the twisted forearm/wrist. Releasing the right hand hold place this hand, fingers on the outside on Uke's forearm directly above your hip. Bear down, increase twist, and keep moving backwards. When Uke is down kneel on the back, grip the forearm with your right hand and start to draw it past your right hip.

14. . . . . Shiho Nage . . . . Variation — Shiho Nage

Assume either posture and check and grip exactly as for Kata Shiho Nage. In either posture, take the left leg towards your front right corner, make tentai and go into kneeling position. If you keep your right arm straight Uke's arm will be bent as you kneel. Depending upon how far you step and turn under the arm you can either drop Uke to his rear or his direct front but the application is best if Uke's arm is held away from his head instead of being folded straight back. Whether you take him forwards or backwards draw your right hand towards your stomach and Uke should make a *rolling breakfall* out of the application. Tori should use his forearm as a bar against Uke's forearm — in effect, pulling with your hand and pushing with your elbow.

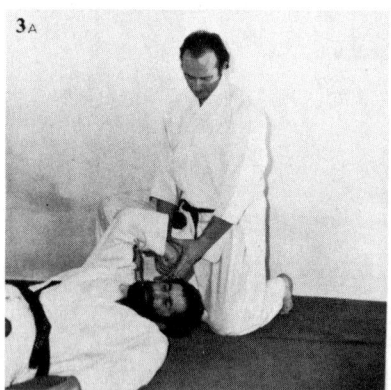

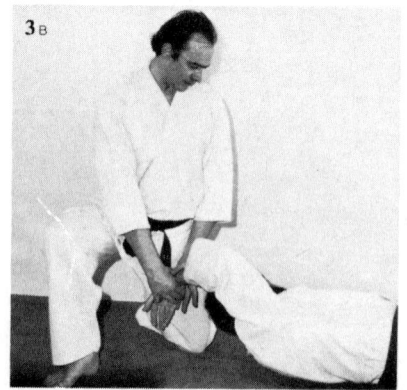

15. . . . . Mae Otoshi . . . . Variation — Mae Otoshi or Uki Goshi

Assume neutral and check attack with hands exactly as for Shiho Nage, but take the left arm under Uke's attacking arm and then take the left hand across the chest. With that left upper arm you can now effect leverage against Uke's elbow. Pivoting on the right foot turn into neutral, 180 degree turn, and inclining your upper body to the right place your left hip in front of Uke. Turn hard right. Uke makes rolling breakfall, and do not forget to release your holds as he goes.

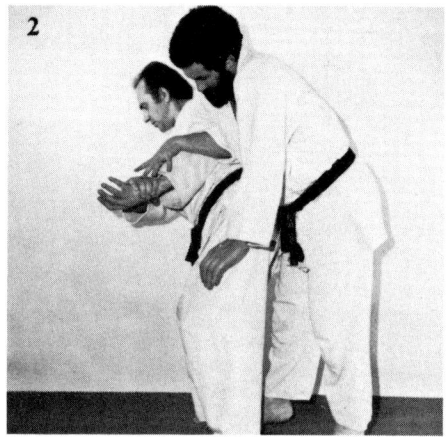

16. . . . . Sumi Otoshi . . . . Variation — Sumi Otoshi or Uki Otoshi

Assume either posture and check/grip as for Kata Sumi Otoshi. Do not attempt to raise at the elbow but take firm grip at Uke's wrist with both hands. Retaining assumed posture drive both hands hard towards Uke's rear corner, applying strong pressure with the right hand.

17. . . . . Hiki Otoshi . . . . Variation – Hiki Otoshi

Assume right posture; without stepping to right as in Kata Hiki Otoshi, make hand checks and grips as for Kata application. Turn left hand grip forwards so that Uke's arm is turned palm uppermost and begin to apply leverage with right hand against elbow. Turn left 180 degrees so that Uke is in your direct rear, take right leg back and between Uke's legs, draw downwards with the left hand and upwards with the right increasing the leverage against the elbow joint. Incline momentum forwards, turning to your left. Uke makes rolling breakfall.

Application is very similar to Judo's Seio Otoshi but in this application leverage is applied against Uke's elbow joint.

IN CONCLUSION

As a result of the preceding pages it may well be that students of this style will have questions to which they would like explicit answers; I can only suggest that they seek answers from their instructors. If that instructor is unable to give a satisfactory answer then seek new tuition as there should not be any question that the competent instructor of this style cannot answer.

It may also come about that some of the as yet uninitiated may take an interest and seek a school — but some guarded advice should be offered. Immediately anything resembling a Martial Art becomes popular 'instructors' come crawling out of the woodwork with cash-till at the ready. Because of the nature of the practice of Aikido — namely it does not have the *physical* appearance of other Martial Arts — it is unlikely that we will see a television series and a glut of motion pictures about Aikido, but there are those who are always too willing to provide a service where they think a service is needed. One cannot draw a conclusive line of advice when it comes to ensuring that the individual receives value for their tuition-money but over the past fourteen years I have taught at a number of clubs and perhaps I can offer some advice based upon those fourteen years.

The prospective beginner is, naturally, very gullible when it comes to seeking a club. He, or she, wants to practise a particular sport and does not really care where or what that club is so long as they can provide the service. They are usually drawn to those clubs who advertise 'qualified instructors' and recognised by such-and-such association or control commission. It does not always follow that if a club is a member of every association, control commission and pseudo organisation going that the instructors of that club know their jobs. Coach awards and the like do not make a competent instructor — and neither do Japanese-recognised grades. So, what do you look for when you seek a club? What should you judge that club by and what type of 'club' should you avoid? Obviously, a club where you will receive competent instruction and where you will be accepted into that club and not made to feel an outsider is the club to seek.

The good club will welcome your inquiries and will usually insist that you visit them and watch a class before accepting you. The good club will have literature available for you to read and it will give you some indication about Aikido, the club and its aims. The Rules and Regulations of that club will be displayed and you will be required to complete an application form before accepting you for the introductory course. If that club does not run a beginners course you will practice on normal practice nights and while the senior class carries out its practice you will be taken to one side and be taught by a senior grade for at least the first four lessons, thereafter you will join in the normal class and be looked after by one of the other grades until the instructor feels that you are competent enough to join in with the rest of the class but you will be under the constant eye of the instructor all the time.

The sincere club will welcome you into the class and will not insist that you join such-and-such organisation; you should be free to have any personal affiliation that you wish. If pressure is brought to bear upon you about joining anything then seek a new club if you have no desire to become involved in inevitable politics.

So, as far as seeking a club and a competent instructor are concerned, shop around and see what you will be getting before you part with a single penny of your money. If you find a club with a good instructor and a happy atmosphere then go in; but keep an open mind. If you hear of any opposition clubs in your area then go and see them, perhaps they might be better than you have been led to believe but above all, always respect the other person's right to practise any style of any Martial Art that they wish and their right to have any or no affiliation loyalties that they desire. *Recognition* is a word that plagues the Martial Arts; over the past fourteen years I have come to the conclusion that recognition is not worth the proverbial rub of soap. A standard of tuition and a standard of practice are not, in my opinion, altered one iota by recognition. A club that boasts *recognition* is one to be avoided. The individual should judge for themselves and if they come across a club where they get enjoyment from their practice and enjoyment from the company of the other practitioners then they have the best club.

The main difference between this style of Aikido and others is the *randori* in this style. There are those who argue that to try and use an Aikido technique against another who is also trying to use an Aikido technique is not true Aikido. But, once again, how does one draw the line? To those who claim that Aikido *is* self-defence I can only say that as a self-defence pure Aikido leaves much to be desired. In a real-life situation matters are not as well controlled as they are in the dojo; the punch is not pulled and the booted-foot hurts when it makes contact. The uneven pavement or the pitted and holed parkland do not allow the smooth foot movements that can be attained on the tatami. The attacker does not have the interests of the *Tori* at heart — and neither does the *Tori* of his *Uke*. If we taught and practised our Aikido as self-defence we would probably have one fatality a day in our dojos, or at least one severe injury — if neither then we could not be practising *real* self-defence! The only way to learn self-preservation is the hard way — on the streets and in the back alleys but bear the old saying in mind, 'look for trouble and you sure as hell find it!' I prefer to accept Aikido as a sport, based upon self-defence.

Of course, one can interpret the term 'sport' in several ways. I do not accept the popular term of sport as being one in which one has to compete against another. I am vehemently *anti* contests and championships. The argument put forward by many is that contest is needed to promote fighting spirit and an ultimate goal. As far as fighting spirit is concerned almost any man will fight if the need arises and one does not have to prostitute a Martial Art in that name and what with the violence on our streets today it would appear that the fighting spirit is something that should be curbed and not encouraged. As for the ultimate goal — a good grading syllabus which calls for a constant improvement in standard and knowledge is all the goal that is needed. We are told that we can never learn it all but I would personally like to try that instead of having a fighting spirit developed and accepting a medal as an ego booster. However, whereas the pro-contest people are entitled to voice their opinions I think those of us who are anti-contest are entitled to voice ours. Perhaps we should decide for ourselves as to what we would like our respective Art to be instead of having opinion do it for us. Unfortunately there are a number, in Aikido, who have similar opinions as I but do not voice them — for fear that they will lose their *recognition* — instead they go along with the decisions made by others which, I believe, are not the opinions of the majority.

I have 'spoken' at some length about the contest-championship aspect in this style because I believe that there are many, both with and without, knowledge of the Tomiki-Style who believe that contest-championship is an integral part of the practice; in fact very similar to present-day Judo. I believe that there should be at least one Martial Art that anyone can practise without the fear that they are going to be drawn into contest work. Agreed, this style has randori which may be only a short step from *shai* but I do not believe that we must do it 'because they do it in Japan'. In fact in Japan, at Waseda, the style of Aikido is changed almost daily! It does not follow that we have to follow suit. To most of us our respective Martial Art is a hobby, something that we take part in after, usually, a day's work. It is not a religion and I do not believe we should allow it to influence our everyday life. Perhaps some of the aspects of Bushido are noble and fine but they do not have a real place in today's world. We therefore have to start to take our Martial Arts in perspective and bring them to a level that we can understand and accept. Agreed, our Martial Arts, for the most part, are Japanese but it does not follow that we have to try and become Japanese for a number of hours per day or week. To the best of my knowledge we 'invented' boxing and soccer — but we most certainly are not the world's best at either of them! The Americans started to box their way and the South Americans started to play their way — perhaps we should start to practise and teach our way?

I have not included a glossary of terms in this book. This may disappoint the reader and student but a complete list of the terminology of this style can be found in *The KOA Dictionary and Guide,* published by Paul H. Crompton Limited. It is a very useful addition to any Budoka's library.

Finally, my thanks to my Uke, Terry Holland and to Doreen White for her competent camera-handling. Over the years they have been my loyalest pupils and friends and my words of appreciation are not really adequate.